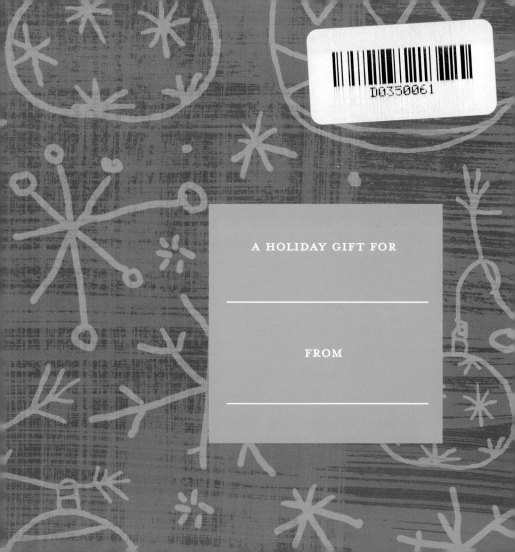

A HOLIDAY GIFT FOR

_____

FROM

_____

Christmas Unwrapped
Lighthearted Humor to Get You Through the Holidays

Copyright © 2003
Hallmark Licensing, Inc.

Published by Hallmark Books, a division of Hallmark Cards, Inc.,
Kansas City, MO 64141
Visit us on the Web at www.hallmark.com.

Editor's Note: Kaopectate® is a registered trademark of Pharmacia.
"Fashion Faux Paws" photograph by Meredith Parmelee.

Designed by Walé Adeniran
Art Director: Mark Cordes

PRINTED IN CHINA

BOK 6019

# CHRISTMAS UNWRAPPED

Lighthearted
Humor
to Get You
Through
the Holidays

by Scott Emmons

# Foreword

It's Christmas! The season
    of tinsel and holly,
When icicles glisten
    and spirits are jolly! ✳
When everyone's cheerful
    and festively dressed,
And – hey, let's be honest –
    a little bit stressed!

The shopping and shipping
    and decking the halls,
The holiday traffic,
    the crowds in the malls,
The cookies to bake
    and the presents to wrap
Can leave you in need
    of a long winter's nap…

So if lines at the post office
fill you with dread
And visions of credit cards
dance in your head,
There's an excellent cure
for your holiday woe—
Just turn it all into
a big Ho-Ho-Ho!
A smile and a snicker
will carry you through,
And that's just what this book
is intended to do!
So take a deep breath
and forget your white knuckles.

Relax and enjoy a few
Christmastime chuckles!
Just grab all the grins
and guffaws you can get,
And make this your merriest
holiday yet!

*Scott Emmons*

# Contents

Counting the Days

Battle in the Burbs

Ad Nauseam

Sausage and Cheese!

Holiday Snooze Letter

Homey Holiday

A Parent's Joy

Christmas Magic

Pet Peeve / Decorating for Dummies

Mystery Card / No Pain, No Angel

The Twelve Weeks of Christmas

Wish List

Dream Tree / A Nod to Nog

Eeee! Shopping!

Gift Thrift / P.O.'d

Grandma's Gift

Greedy Guests

Miss Perfect

Hidden Treasure / Merry Christmess!

Energy Crisis / Maim That Tune

Location, Location, Location / Picture — Perfect

All I Want for Christmas

Heads Up

Fashion Faux Paws / Toy Joy

Holiday Observance

The Tree and Me

Expiration Date

Post Haste

Wrap Flap / Secret Ingredient

The Mall at Christmas

What Was I Thinking

Christmas Conundrum

Treats, Glorious Treats!

Hefty Holidays

We Wish You a Something, Something…

Morning Madness

Fond Farewell

A Parting Wish

## COUNTING THE DAYS

They're counting the days
until Christmas,
As sugarplums dance
in their heads.
They're staying up
later and later.
They can hardly stay tucked
in their beds.
They've rigged up a sleigh
just like Santa's,
And they're hitching up
poor little Rover.
They're counting the days
until Christmas.
I'm counting the days
till it's over!

## BATTLE IN THE BURBS

Last year my neighbor Bob displayed
     a wreath upon his door.
It looked a little bare,
     and so he wanted something more.
He hung a string of lights
     to make the festive mood complete,
Which caught the jealous eye
     of Old Man Potts across the street.
Now Potts was sour and cranky,
     not the jolliest of guys.
You could see his cutthroat nature
     in his cold and steely eyes.
And when he saw what Bob had done,
     he hung a bigger wreath
     with fancy frosted pinecones
     and a velvet bow beneath.

He decked his lawn with ornamental
reindeer and a sleigh,
Then added flashing lights
that really clobbered Bob's display!
But Bob would not accept defeat—
he really looked alive!
And soon a whole Nativity
appeared out on his drive.
The Kings upon their camels,
with their faithful entourage,
Were guided by a gleaming star
on top of Bob's garage.
A host of plastic shepherds
kept their flocks upon his lawn.
"Take that!" he yelled across the street,
and Potts yelled, "Bring it on!"
The gloves were off, and now those two
put on a frightful show.

*The battle continues…*

Their lights made downtown Vegas
look like Podunk, Idaho!
There were choirs of angels, toiling elves,
and blinking candy canes.
There were heaps of gift-wrapped boxes
hauled by working model trains.
There were polystyrene snowmen
standing ninety-one feet tall.
There were motor-driven Santas
shouting, "Merry Christmas, all!"
There were huge, majestic Christmas trees
that towered to the sky.
But even up to Christmas Eve,
their contest was a tie.
So Bob and Potts stood on their lawns,
each glaring at his foe,
Declaring he would not give in—
till it began to snow!
Now dreaming of white Christmases

has never been my style,
But once that blizzard started up,
   I couldn't help but smile.
It covered every ornament,
      it silenced every bell,
It buried every reindeer
      and each tiny elf as well.
It squelched those shouting Santas,
      and it dimmed each garish light
Till everything was peaceful
      in an endless sea of white.
And then poor Bob and Old Man Potts,
   who'd battled tooth and claw,
Could only shake each other's hands
   and call the thing a draw.
And as for me, I made a vow
   by which I still abide.
Whenever Christmas rolls around,
   I hang my wreath inside!

## AD NAUSEAM

Christmas ads, Christmas ads

on my TV set,

They come fast and furious,

and they're not stopping yet!

My brain is overloaded,

and my patience sorely taxed.

Those ad guys won't be happy

till my credit cards are maxed!

# SAUSAGE AND CHEESE!

I have an Aunt Sadie.
    I've met her just twice.
I don't know her well,
    But she seems very nice.
And at holiday time,
    Being eager to please,
She sends an assortment
    Of sausage and cheese.

Sausage and cheese!
    Sausage and cheese!
A yearly assortment
    Of sausage and cheese!

I sampled them once,
    And the cheeses, I think,
Were flavored with lye
    And industrial ink.
One taste of the meats
Brought me down to my knees.
    I just about choked
On that sausage and cheese!

Sausage and cheese!
        Sausage and cheese!
That foul and unsavory
        Sausage and cheese!

    So now every year
  When the package comes in,
I don't waste a second—
        It goes in the bin.
  Then a note to my aunt
        Puts my conscience at ease:
"Merry Christmas, and thanks
        For the sausage and cheese!"

Sausage and cheese!
        Sausage and cheese!
  That truly incredible,
        Awful, inedible,
Well-meaning present
        Of sausage and cheese!

# HOLIDAY SNOOZE LETTER

A photocopied note arrives
     from Ted, a dear old friend—
The newsy Christmas letter
     that he never fails to send.
He says he's doing very well.
     The family's fine, the pets are swell.
There's just a ton of stuff to tell
     Before the note can end!

It's been a super year, says Ted.
     His stocks are on the rise.
His wife Lorraine's a shoo-in
     For her second Nobel Prize.
They've bought a new vacation home
A twenty-minute drive from Rome,
     No bigger than the Astrodome—
     "A very modest size."

Ted Junior's now at Harvard Law
And earning solid A's,
While Buffy's getting bigger roles
In major Broadway plays.
Young Tommy, at the age of nine,
Is helping NASA crews refine
An innovative new design
For outerspace cafés.

The note continues on and on
About their grand pursuits,
Their lofty dreams, their noble goals,
Their labor and its fruits.
I finish up and, with a sigh,
Begin my rather terse reply:
"Next time you pile it up *this* high,
Include a pair of boots!"

## HOMEY HOLIDAY

I'll be home for Christmas
(I go there every year),

A place that's plain and peaceful

with a cheery atmosphere,

Where winter skies are silvery

and days are cold and sleety.

I'll be home for Christmas

'cause I can't afford Tahiti.

# A PARENT'S JOY

Each year when Christmas rolls around,

My happy heart begins to soar

To see the stockings hanging up

Instead of crumpled on the floor.

# Christmas Magic

"Some day," I'll see a reindeer herd

go soaring overhead.

A gentle Christmas snow will fall

in shades of green and red.

I'll see a snowman come to life

and start to celebrate.

And on that strange, enchanted day…

my tree will stand up straight.

## PET PEEVE

I'd rather eat
    a reindeer whole
Or have my stocking
    stuffed with coal
Or perch upon
    a blazing log
Or drink an egg
    without the nog
Or skinny-dip
    where Santa dwells
Than hear a dog sing
    JINGLE BELLS!

## DECORATING FOR DUMMIES

I hope you'll heed this good advice
and not just try to wing it.
I've found it's best to *pop* the corn
before you try to string it!

### MYSTERY CARD

I just got a card from a lady named Kay.
Have I ever met her? I really can't say.
Perhaps she's a neighbor
or someone at work.
A classmate from high school?
The video clerk?
I simply can't place her.
My brain's at a loss.
But she just might be someone
I don't want to cross.
So I'm mailing a card
in my own thoughtful way
With warm Christmas greetings
for someone named Kay.

## No Pain, No Angel

I made an angel
in the snow
Just like the little
children do.
I'm glad I made it,
even though
My poor old buns
are frozen through!

# THE TWELVE WEEKS OF CHRISTMAS

I know these decorations well,

the holly and the tree…

These silver bells

and Christmas wreaths

are like old friends to me.

And when I stop to wonder why,

it makes me kind of sober

To think they've all

been in the mall

since early in October.

## WISH LIST

Dear Santa,

Toys get broken.
　　Candy's cheap.
Pets take effort.
　　Fruit won't keep.
Candles smell.
　　Clothes might clash.
Games are boring.
　　Please bring cash.

Love,
mindy

## DREAM TREE

I think that I shall never see

A fresh and well-

proportioned tree

That doesn't shed and doesn't ooze

For less than

eighty smackeroos.

## A Nod to Nog

Eggnog is

for those who think

A triple shake's

too light a drink!

## Eeee! Shopping!

For Christmas this year,

I went shopping online.

The presents were perfect.

The prices were fine.

In fact, my delight

with the gifts that I bought

May almost make up

for the virus I caught!

## GIFT THRIFT

For saving cash at Christmastime,

I've got a special knack.

When someone says "You shouldn't have,"

I take my present back!

P.O.'d

Fred the friendly snowman

was a happy, merry fellow.

But lately

Fred's been seeing red

since Bowser

turned him yellow.

## GRANDMA'S GIFT

Which present came from Grandma?

It isn't hard to see.

The gift wrap is the same she's used

since 1943.

# GREEDY GUESTS

The relatives like country ham
        Plus all the turkey they can get.
They put away a leg of lamb.
        They've barely started yet!

They eat a heap of stuffing then,
        A pound or two — or three or four,
And then devour a Cornish hen.
        Which leaves them wanting more.

They scan the room with hungry eyes
        For cookies, cakes, and sugarplums.
They stuff themselves with mincemeat pies
        And lick up all the crumbs.

They finish up with half a ton
        Of candy canes — they like the crunch.
And when their Christmas breakfast's done,
        They sit and dream of lunch.

## Miss Perfect

Melinda McGinty's a Christmas sensation.
Her energy level's incredibly high.
Her cards are mailed out by the first of November.
She's done with her shopping by early July.

She makes the most marvelous holiday cookies
And gingerbread houses in various styles.
She's known for her handcrafted marzipan Santas.
"It wouldn't be Christmas without them," she smiles.

Melinda McGinty won't rest for a minute
When striving for maximum holiday cheer.
She settles for nothing but outright perfection.
I'm tempted to spit in her eggnog this year!

## HIDDEN TREASURE

We got this lamp from Auntie Jane
    one Christmas long ago.
It's sort of like a walrus head
    with lion's feet below.
We never know just what to say
    when people ask, "What is it?"
That's why we only bring it out
    when Auntie comes to visit.

I've seen some frightful Christmas scenes:

Ornaments in smithereens,

Needles scattered wall to wall,

Tinsel trailing down the hall,

Angels fallen from their heights,

Knotted up cords and shattered lights,

Branches turned to mangled sticks…

Cats and Christmas trees don't mix!

## ENERGY CRISIS

I've lost my mind! My brain has cracked!

I must have been deluded

To think a Christmas toy would come

With batteries included!

## MAIM THAT TUNE

There's a song that they never stop playin',

    A side-splittin', knee-slappin' zinger,

'Bout a reindeer that ran over Grandma.

    I wish he had aimed for the singer!

## LOCATION, LOCATION, LOCATION!

Today I saw a winter scene

too striking to ignore.

I've never seen a snowman

with a carrot *there* before!

## PICTURE-PERFECT

When Junior sits on Santa's lap,

avoid a common error

And take your snapshot well before

he starts to scream in terror.

# ALL I WANT FOR CHRISTMAS

The carolers are singing.

"Merry Christmas!" someone yells.

The city streets are ringing

with the clang of Christmas bells.

Yes, everywhere the air is filled

with sounds of joy and mirth.

But all I want for Christmas

is a little peace on Earth.

## HEADS UP

Christmastime is now upon us.

'Tis the season to beware!

Keep your guard up every minute.

Danger's lurking everywhere!

Take precautions. Don't get careless.

Anywhere you chance to go,

Keep one eye on what's above you.

*Always* check for mistletoe!

## Fashion Faux Paws

You who dress

    your dogs and cats

In cutesy coats

    and Santa hats,

Give me just

    a little clue…

What did Fluffy

    do to YOU?

## TOY JOY

My eyes are blurred, my brain is mush,
My hands begin to tremble.
I fell for those deceitful words:
"Easy to assemble!"

## HOLIDAY OBSERVANCE

Observing crowds in shopping malls

is more than just a silly game.

It offers proof beyond a doubt

that no two flakes

are quite the same!

## THE TREE AND ME

O Christmas tree, O Christmas tree,

You stand so proud and tall,

As I would do if I could keep

*my* bad side to the wall!

## Expiration Date

When it comes to tasteful home decor,
the leading experts say
A Christmas tree should not stay up
much past the end of May.

I WANTED TO SEND
YOU SOMETHING
EXTRA SPECIAL FOR
CHRISTMAS . . .

VIA AIR MAIL

SPECIAL DELIVERY

HANDLE
WITH
CARE

## POST HASTE

I'm shipping my presents

by SuperExpress.

They should be delivered

in two days or less.

It's not that I dawdled,

I want you to know.

I got in this line

over three weeks ago!!!

## WRAP FLAP

It's hard to stay cheerful and jolly,

Or even to keep self-control,

When you need a few inches

of clear plastic tape

And you can't find the end of the roll!

## SECRET INGREDIENT

It's said that a group of inventors

    at a lab out in Upper Montclair

Have developed a chemical compound,

    a secret they guard with great care.

Some say it's a rubberlike resin

    with an extract of dragonfly wings,

And it's sold to the makers of fruitcake

    for producing those little red things.

# THE MALL AT CHRISTMAS

The festive lights are twinkling.

The scent of pine is thick.

The tiny tots are lining up

to visit old Saint Nick.

There's a ting-a-ling of sleigh bells

As a chorus sweetly sings.

And if you find a parking spot,

an angel gets its wings!

## WHAT WAS I THINKING?

I bought this ugly ornament.

I don't know why, I must admit.

I'll leave it in the box, I guess,

'Cause hanging's

much too good for it!

## SEEING SANTA

He looked like a peddler just opening his pack...
And a lot like a plumber as seen from the back!

## Christmas Conundrum

I frequently find myself asking

    (though it's not like it keeps me awake)

Why Christmas gives so many people

    a neurotic compulsion to bake!

## Treats, Glorious Treats!

Candy canes and gingerbread!

Christmas cookies, green and red!

Roasted chestnuts! Spicy cheese!

Pass the Kaopectate, please!

## HEFTY HOLIDAYS

I diet all year long, and my will is pretty strong,
But the Christmas season always makes it weak.
This year again, no doubt, all my shameless pigging out
Will reward me with a Santa Claus physique!

How I love those Christmas pies. I prefer them supersize!
I can gobble figgy pudding by the pound.
Every chocolate-covered cherry is a treat to make me merry.
I'll eat *fruitcake* if there's nothing else around!

After New Year I'll be good, eating only what I should.
By the spring I'll shed my extra pounds, and then...
When December rears its head, with its cakes and gingerbread,
I'll give in, of course, and do it all again!

# WE WISH YOU A SOMETHING, SOMETHING...

Here we come a-caroling

    around the neighborhood.

We haven't had a lot of time

    to practice like we should.

We're jolly and we're merry

    and we sing like little birds.

We sure would sound delightful

    if we'd only learned the words!

# MORNING MADNESS

The kids scramble in at the break of the morning.
They dive for the bounty that's under the tree.
The paper, the bows, and the ribbons go flying
And settle in colorful heaps of debris.
"All right!" cries a voice. "A Galactic Avenger!"
"No way!" yells another. "A Malibu Sue!"
And every few seconds, a package is opened
To bring yet another new toy into view.
There are kickboxing robots and tiny green soldiers,
Harmonicas, jump ropes, remote-control cars,
Bicycles, tricycles, spy-vision goggles,
Collectible beanbags! Electric guitars!
There are video games in the latest editions!
Mechanical animals, modeling clay,
And weird little creatures that chirp at each other.
(They'll pick up your language, so watch what you say!)
And then, when the frenzy is over at last
And you swear you bought every last toy in the mall,
The kids turn around with an injured expression
And ask in a whimpering tone, "Is that all???"

# FOND FAREWELL

It's sad to see the day arrive

for taking down the tree.

We'd love to see it linger,

but it isn't meant to be.

Yet in a sense, we never lose

the friend we hold so dear.

The needles in the carpet

will be with us through the year.

# A Parting Wish

May your season be jolly,

  Your halls decked with holly,

  Your ornaments festive and shiny.

May your shopping be quick,

  May your eggnog be thick,

  May your fruitcake be ever so tiny!

May your feast be extensive

  (And not too expensive),

  Your carols a treat for the ears.

May your candles be bright,

  May your spirits be light,

May it be your best Christmas in years!

During the Christmas buying season, shoppers in the United States use their Visa cards an average of 5,340 times a minute. And that's just ONE credit card!

At last count, Americans were buying more than 37 million Christmas trees a year, with about 9 million coming from the 5,000 "choose and cut" farms.

While North American children are hanging stockings at Christmas, Dutch children are setting out shoes to be filled with gifts and treats. They allow more time for filling the shoes...from mid-November to St. Nichola's birthday on December 5.

The movie version of *How the Grinch Stole Christmas* brilliantly features more than 52,000 Christmas lights, about 8,200 ornaments, and nearly 2,000 candy canes.

In 1996, two Florida malls banned Christmas caroling because shoppers and merchants complained that they were too loud and took up too much space. (Scrooges!)

The first Christmas ornaments were homemade paper flowers or apples, biscuits, and sweets.

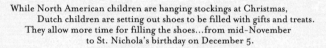

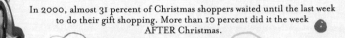

Neither rain nor sleet nor lack of personnel... So many people were sending their homemade Christmas cards in 1822 that the Washington, D.C., postmaster feared the postal service couldn't handle the volume. His solution? Limit the number of cards a person could send! As it turned out, 16 extra employees had to be hired.

In 2000, almost 31 percent of Christmas shoppers waited until the last week to do their gift shopping. More than 10 percent did it the week AFTER Christmas.

Mistletoe was, at one time, so revered and considered so sacred by the Britons that it had to be cut with a golden sickle.

In medieval England, one favored Christmas celebration featured a 165-pound pie made from 2 bushels of flour, 20 pounds of butter, 4 geese, 2 rabbits, 4 wild ducks, 2 woodcocks, 6 snipes (where did they find them?), 4 partridges, 2 neats' tongues, 2 curlews, 6 pigeons, and 7 blackbirds. (Kind of the "meat lovers pizza" of the day.)

Almost 2 billion candy canes are made each year during the Christmas/Hanukkah season.

## ABOUT THE AUTHOR

Scott Emmons is known in the poetry scene
As a genuine, bonafide rhyming machine!
He rhymes in his e-mails, he rhymes in his faxes,
He rhymes on the forms when he's filing his taxes.
He rhymes to be silly, he rhymes to be deep.
His wife even tells us he rhymes in his sleep!
So at Christmas he rhymes in his usual style
In hopes of inspiring a holiday smile!

If you have enjoyed this book,

Hallmark would love

to hear from you.

Please send your comments

to Book Feedback,

2501 McGee, Mail Drop 489,

Kansas City, MO 64141-6580.

Or e-mail us at

booknotes@hallmark.com